Thomas H. Troeger

The End of Preaching

Abingdon Press
Nashville

THE END OF PREACHING

Copyright © 2018 by Abingdon Press

This book is printed on acid-free paper.

Library of Congress Cataloging-in-Publication Data has been requested.

978-1-5018-6809-2

18 19 20 21 22 23 24 25 26 27—10 9 8 7 6 5 4 3 2 1

MANUFACTURED IN THE UNITED STATES OF AMERICA

Praise for *The End of Preaching*

"Poet, hymn writer, master preacher, creative teacher—Tom Troeger fills all of these roles and more, and his many gifts are on rich display in this splendid meditation on preaching. In a world where language is often hollowed out and pressed into the service of marketing and manipulation, it is a deep refreshment to be guided by this wise book toward a way of preaching that finds its proper end in prayer."

—Thomas G. Long, Bandy Professor Emeritus of Preaching, Candler School of Theology, Emory University, Atlanta, GA

"*The End of Preaching* is poetic, profound, and practical. It invites preachers to embark on 'the heart's pilgrimage,' a journey into a preaching life that lives and moves and has its being in prayer. It offers a transformative clarity on both the purpose and the process of preaching that infuses perfunctory preaching with poetic, prayerful passion. It invites preachers and people alike to partake of the 'Church's Banquet,' God's gift of prayer, to be fed and filled to do the church's work of nourishing the world. I look forward to recommending *The End of Preaching* to colleagues and students!"

—Alyce M. McKenzie, Le Van Professor of Preaching and Worship; Altshuler Distinguished Teaching Professor; director, Center for Preaching Excellence; Perkins School of Theology, Southern Methodist University, Dallas, TX

"Classic Troeger! Begins with what seems a modest claim—until pressed toward profound articularity and deep poetic soul!"

—Eugene L. Lowry, William K. McElvaney Professor Emeritus of Preaching, Saint Paul School of Theology, Kansas City, MO; author; jazz musician

"Tom Troeger he describes prayer not as pleading for answers or satisfaction but as a means to be understood. This book has already informed my teaching as I approach first-year students considering vocational outcomes of their theological education. It is a resource that inspires, informs, and encourages all who approach the practice of preaching with insight and honesty."

—Tanya Linn Bennett, associate dean for vocation and formation, associate professor in the practice of public theology and vocation, Drew University, Madison, NJ

"In his own inimitably creative and lucid way, Thomas Troeger has written one of the best books possible on the deep connection between preaching and public worship. Troeger shows how preaching thrives in a climate saturated with public and communal prayers and finds its 'end' in the deep spiritual pilgrimage these prayers create and nurture."

—John S. McClure, Charles G. Finney Professor of Preaching and Worship, Vanderbilt Divinity School, Vanderbilt University, Nashville, TN

"The poetry comes off the page in this lovely, lively little book. Do not be fooled by its slim lines or its elegance. This is a blockbuster. And just the kind of help every praying preacher needs. Which is to say, every preacher."
—Jana Childers, dean, professor of homiletics, San Francisco Theological Seminary, San Anselmo, CA

"Homiletical legend Thomas Troeger, has done us all a favor by leading us back to the alpha and omega of preaching—prayer. Troeger reminds us that if the true end of preaching is prayer, before a preacher is a poet, pastor, or prophet, the preacher is a pray-er. This book is a call to prayer and will guide you to embrace the pulpit as an altar."
—Luke A. Powery, dean, Duke University Chapel; associate professor of homiletics, Duke Divinity School, Duke University, Durham, NC

"With a poet's passion, Troeger leads us into deep recesses of devotion by claiming 'the end of preaching is prayer.' This book turns the duty of preaching into a dance of delight with language, with Creation, with God."
—Richard F. Ward, Fred B Craddock Professor of Homiletics and Worship, Phillips Theological Seminary, Tulsa, OK

"In this lovely adaptation of Tom Troeger's 2016 Beecher Lectures, we are invited to enter the 'temple' with him and to move around in words that conjure what preaching might be like when its end is prayer. The play on words in the title is both a good 'hook' and makes a profound point—as any good preacher will appreciate. The 'end' of preaching Troeger points to is not its demise but its purpose and power. What is the *end*, the response, the change wrought in human lives and communities through preaching? This book has reminded me of why I do what I do, provided me with a new framework for the work of preaching, and deeply nourished me for the continued journey."
—Ginger E. Gaines-Cirelli, senior pastor, Foundry United Methodist Church, Washington, DC

"Do not be fooled by the brevity of this book. Like a great poem, it is packed with beauty and provocation that far exceeds its word count. In presenting prayer (metaphorically and literally) as the end of preaching, Troeger will inspire readers to celebrate and rethink the work they do in the pulpit each week. This is a must-read for preachers who care about the art and purpose of preaching."
—O. Wesley Allen, Jr., Lois Craddock Perkins Professor of Homiletics, Perkins School of Theology, Southern Methodist University, Dallas, TX

Contents

Foreword

Some preachers wonder whether we are living in end times, as far as preaching is concerned. "The end of preaching" could describe the sermon's quiet exit to the wings of cultural importance or relevance: a kind of slow fade. A long goodbye.

But Thomas Troeger sees the end of preaching as a starting point for spirited reflection. With his trademark elegance and precision, and with joyful enthusiasm that fairly dances off the page, he invites us to explore the worlds that open when we ask old questions in a new key: what *is* the end—the purpose—of preaching? Where does it all lead? When the sermon is over, when worship is done, what do we hope will happen in the bodies, minds, and souls of the hearers? What comes next—for them, and for the church?

These are essential questions, eternal questions, and ones that every preacher (and Beecher lecturer) must wrestle with sooner or later. Troeger takes delight in how many before him have pondered them: "Preaching is for the care of souls...the saving of souls...the liberation of captives...the proclamation of gospel." But he, in his turn, takes us straight to the heart of things: *Praying's the end of preaching.*

Foreword

These lectures are such a gift. Reading them is like drinking from the purest of mountain streams and slaking a thirst we didn't know we had. Troeger is that rare combination of preacher and poet, teacher and scholar: he greets the universe with endless curiosity and wonder and tenderness. The breadth and depth of his knowledge is truly astonishing, as the range of conversation partners in these lectures shows. And he has the wisdom of decades spent walking alongside his students, listening to their sermons. Troeger has learned a few things, in his time, about this magnificent foolishness, this holy act that keeps many of us sprinting after grace and up all night. He's contemplated the end of preaching. That he continues to set the bar for imaginative homiletical theology is our gain and our inspiration.

If you are weary of preaching's weight, if you are tired of the promise of quick fixes and cheap grace, this is your book. Read it and be renewed. Read it and be empowered. Read it and join the banquet in the temple, as Troeger sings to us the refrain, from the closing lines of the book:

If the end of preaching is prayer, then how will we arrive at that end? The only way to arrive there is to begin there. The end of preaching is prayer, and the beginning of preaching is prayer.

Anna Carter Florence

Chapter One

"The Church's Banquet"

Why preach? What is the purpose of it all?

Whether you are just beginning to preach or you are a longtime experienced preacher, how you answer this question will have an immense impact in shaping all of your sermons: If you are starting out and you have no clear goal in mind, you may mistakenly conclude that good preaching is simply a matter of mastering effective methods of communication. Or if you have preached for years but have lost sight of your initial homiletical vision and passion, preparing a sermon may have become a burdensome weekly task.

If someone asked you to finish the following sentence: "The end of preaching is…," what would you answer?

Would you say "The end of preaching is to bring people to faith in God?"

Or

"The end of preaching is to proclaim the good news of Jesus Christ."

Or

"The end of preaching is to transform people's lives."

Or

"The end of preaching is to save sinners."

Or

"The end of preaching is to teach people sound theology."

Or

"The end of preaching is the pastoral care of the congregation."

Or

"The end of preaching is to illuminate a text from the Bible."

Or

"The end of preaching is to awaken compassion and establish justice."

Even though all of these are perfectly fine ways to complete the sentence, they do not begin to exhaust the possibilities! There are endless ways to complete the sentence that begins "The end of preaching is..."

Take a moment before you read any further and complete the sentence, "The end of preaching is..."

Write it down so that you can use it as a starting point for a dialogue with all that follows.

One of the most famous preachers in American history, Henry Ward Beecher (1813–1887) considered it essential that every preacher have a clear idea of the purpose of preaching. Beecher gave the first three years of the Yale lecture series named in honor of his father, Lyman Beecher. Shortly into the start of his first lecture, on January 31, 1872, Beecher reflects:

> It is hardly an imaginary case to describe one as approaching the Sabbath day somewhat in this way: "O dear me, I have got to preach! I have

beat out pretty much all there is in that straw, and I wonder what I shall preach on next"; and so the man takes the Bible and commences to turn over the leaves, hoping that he will hit something. He looks up and down, and turns forward and backward, and finally he does see a light, and he says, "I can make something interesting from that." Interesting, why? For what purpose?...He is a perfunctory preacher, doing a duty because appointed to that duty.[1]

Turning from the Pinhole of Our Immediate Curiosity

Beecher's affirmation of the need for clarity about the purpose of preaching found ringing affirmation from the ranks of Beecher lecturers that followed him. "Why preach? What is the purpose of it all?" are questions that reach across the generations of outstanding preachers. The great preachers knew the questions cannot be ignored. In 1947 Batsell Barrett Baxter published a book gathering together substantial quotations from nearly all the Beecher lectures that had been delivered up to that time. Baxter ties the citations together with his own observations and analytical summaries. He notes: "Twenty-one of the Lyman Beecher speakers discussed in their lectures the importance of thoughtful consideration of the purpose of the sermon. The feeling was unanimous that a proper realization of the purpose for which the sermon is to be preached is essential to success in the pulpit. There was no dissenting voice on this point."[2]

1. Henry Ward Beecher, *Yale Lectures on Preaching*, three volumes in one (New York: Fords, Howard, & Hulbert, 1892), vol. I, 4–5. The pagination begins anew with each volume.
2. Batsell Barrett Baxter, *The Heart of the Yale Lectures* (New York: The Macmillan Company, 1947), 231.

No lecturer was more adamant about the matter than J. H. Jowett who insisted: "Let us clearly formulate the end at which we aim. Let us put it into words. Don't let it hide in the cloudy realm of vague assumptions. Let us arrest ourselves in the very midst of our assumptions, and compel ourselves to name and register our ends."[3]

R. W. Dale, in his Beecher lectures published in 1890, summarizes the spirit of this homiletical concern with an aphorism: "We shall preach to no purpose unless we have a purpose in preaching."[4]

What then is the end of preaching for Beecher and for some of the representative lecturers who follow him? I will briefly explore this question because I want to frame my own contribution to the purpose of preaching with the history of homiletics during the last century and a half as it is manifest in the Beecher lectures, probably the most famous and significant lecture series in homiletics in English. We live in a digital age that has the unfortunate tendency to reinforce an ahistorical perspective on reality. As Maria Bustillos observes: "Reading on-screen tempts us to see things only through the pinhole of our immediate curiosity."[5] I hope my historical citations will expand our perspective beyond "the pinhole of our immediate curiosity" to a sense of the larger trajectory that the Beecher lectures provide.

Before I quote Beecher on the purpose of preaching, I note that we may sometimes cringe at his antiquated idiom of heavily masculine expression. His was not an age of inclusive language. Despite the masculine bias of his speech, Beecher asserts in the course of his lectures:

---

3. Baxter, *The Heart of the Yale Lectures*, 237–38, originally appeared in J. H. Jowett, *The Preacher: His Life and Work* (New York: Hodder & Stoughton, 1912), 147–48.
4. Baxter, *The Heart of the Yale Lectures*, 236. The quotation originally appears in R. W. Dale, *Nine Lectures on Preaching* (London: Hodder & Stoughton, 1890), 131.
5. Maria Bustillos, "The Oxford English Dictionary," *The New York Times Magazine* (July 5, 2015): 23.

"I believe in women speaking praying in meetings, as well as preaching and lecturing and voting. ... I feel that the church has lost one half of its best power in the exclusion of sisterhood from speaking in our meetings."[6]

What, then, is the end of preaching for Beecher? In his lecture of February 1, 1872, Beecher gets at the purpose of preaching by naming how it differs from mere eloquence. He says: "Eloquence has been defined, sometimes, as the art of moving men by speech. Preaching has this additional quality, that it is the art of moving men from a lower to a higher life. It is the art of inspiring them toward a nobler manhood."[7]

In his second series of lectures, under a section subtitled "The Function of the Pulpit," Beecher asserts "the great duty of the ministry ... is ... to give a *soul* to the great working, thinking, throbbing world."[8]

In his third series of lectures Beecher is boldly christological in stating the end of preaching: "It is the living, personal Christ ... who ought to be the end and object of your ministry."[9] Beecher underlines and expands this statement near the end of his final lecture series: "We are to labor to bring [people] to the stature of the fullness of manhood in Christ Jesus. That is the supreme end of the Christian ministry."[10]

A nobler humanity, giving soul to the world, bringing people to a mature relationship with Christ: these are three of the major themes in Beecher's understanding of the end of preaching. But it would not surprise Beecher to find that those who followed him, shaped by the circumstances of their own historical context, would express the

6. Beecher, *Yale Lectures on Preaching*, vol. II, 66–67.
7. Beecher, *Yale Lectures on Preaching*, vol. I, 29.
8. Beecher, *Yale Lectures on Preaching*, vol. II, 31. Emphasis is Beecher's.
9. Beecher, *Yale Lectures on Preaching*, vol. III, 156.
10. Beecher, *Yale Lectures on Preaching*, vol. III, 283.

end of preaching in idioms that addressed a changed and changing world. Beecher placed his own lectures in this dynamic understanding of history:

> In our day, the style of theology has changed. You will be compelled to change with it. There are great causes at work, quite independent of mere individual volition. Men tell us we must go back again and pursue the old sound doctrinal system; but you cannot get back.... That which fitted the condition of men earlier than our time does not fit our time, and has been, or is being, sloughed off.[11]

Consider then a few representative voices who followed Beecher, delivering their lectures decades after he told his own generation of preachers they would be "compelled to change." Note especially how much the historical context shapes each preacher's vision of the purpose of preaching. Let this observation awaken you to how your time and place in history shape your understanding of why you preach.

William Fraser McDowell presented his lectures during the academic year 1916–1917 in the midst of World War I. For him, the end of preaching is to engage a shattered world, a world he describes in these words: "Men are wondering, as they have in other periods, whether Christianity is a living or a spent force in the world. The faith of many is in eclipse. Many walk in despair and darkness. They feel that one world is dead, they are not sure that a better has any power to be born. Into such an era you come."[12]

In the academic year of 1942–1943, while World War II is raging, Paul Scherer attests that for him preaching has a single, focused end:

---

11. Beecher, *Yale Lectures on Preaching*, vol. II, 147–48.
12. Baxter, *The Heart of the Yale Lectures*, 10. The quotation originally appeared in William Fraser McDowell, *Good Ministers of Jesus Christ* (New York: Abingdon, 1918), 20.

I mean to make everything subservient to one purpose, and that purpose [is] not the writing of a great sermon or the elaboration of some mighty and puissant theme, but the ministering to human souls of the redemptive power of God. Do bear that forever in mind.... You are preaching not to make clear what good preaching is or ought to be; you are preaching to lay hold desperately on life, broken life, hurt life, soiled life, staggering life, helpless life, hard, cynical, indifferent, willful life, to lay hold on it with both hands in the high name of the Lord Christ and to lift it toward his dream.[13]

All of the lecturers I have cited to this point are only available in print. I did not have the advantage of seeing the speakers' faces, observing their body language, and hearing the timbre and inflection of their voices—all factors that reach to the heart in ways that words alone do not. Henry Ward Beecher himself understood the importance of the physical bearing of a speaker upon the effectiveness of communication. In his first series of lectures, Beecher observes: "A man's whole form is a part of his public speaking. His feet speak and so do his hands. You put a man in one of these barreled pulpits, where there is no responsibility laid upon him as to his body, and he falls into all manner of gawky attitudes, and rests himself like a country horse at a hitching-post."[14]

Fortunately, I have had the gift of hearing and seeing several Beecher lecturers over the last decade, and I can report none of them rested themselves like a country horse at a hitching post! Tapes of their vocal inflections, gestures, and facial expressions are running in my memory as I recount their varied purposes of preaching.[15]

---

13. Baxter, *The Heart of the Yale Lectures,* 238. The quotation originally appears in Paul Scherer, *For We Have This Treasure* (New York: Harper & Brothers, 1944), 181.

14. Beecher, *Yale Lectures on Preaching,* vol. I, 71.

15. All of the Beecher lectures that I cite from 2008 onward can be viewed online at www.divinity.yale.edu by clicking on the "connect with us" link.

In 2008 Renita Weems announces the purpose of preaching in the very title she gives to her lectures: "Preaching Against the Grain: Recovering the Voices of Those from the Underside of History."

In 2011 Brian Blount compares the apocalyptic world of John with the apocalyptic character of the current state of society and asserts:

> Our homiletical task then is to overcome our modern and postmodern skittishness [about apocalypticism] and to proclaim the contemporary relevance of this imminent dawn of the dead through the revealing lens of both religious and secular apocalyptic eschatology. We begin by preaching in ways that challenge our current world view, in ways that force us to see that we human ones are not in charge of the world we call our own, that we are in the midst of a crisis we do not fully comprehend.[16]

In 2012 Anna Carter Florence, adapting language that she learned in an undergraduate course on theater, grounds the purpose of preaching in the creative exploration of the scriptures. She exhorts preachers: "Set us loose with the biblical texts. Tell us to go and rehearse one together. And show us when you found something true and we'll see and we'll talk and rework whatever happened and somehow through a power that is never our own we will see God and so ourselves more deeply and true than we could ever do on our own."

In 2014 Otis Moss III makes a distinction between two different kinds of preaching—"blue note preaching" and "the gospel shout." He asserts: "If we are to reclaim the best of the preaching tradition then we must learn what I call a blue note gospel. Before you get to your resurrection shout you must pass by the challenge and pain of Calvary.... Blues is the foundation of preaching."

---

16. All the citations from my tenure at Yale, 2005–2015, are taken from video recordings of the Beecher lectures available on the Yale Divinity School website.

Had I world enough and time to present from all of the 150 Beecher lecturers who have preceded me, it would make dramatically clear what these brief excerpts suggest: Namely, there are numberless ways to complete the statement "The end of preaching is...," and they change continually as the historical context changes.

A Deceptively Simple Statement

Nevertheless, I will now focus entirely on a single end of preaching. It may not be the end of preaching that you wrote down, but it is broad and deep enough that you can hold it in conversation with the end you have named. And in the process you will refine and clarify why you preach.

The end I have chosen is not original with me. I am taking it from George Herbert's great collection of sacred poems, *The Temple*. Several years ago I reread *The Temple*, a work that I had first studied as a sophomore in college. George Herbert (1593–1633) was a priest and pastor. Most literary critics consider Herbert to be one of the greatest Christian poets in the English language.

The poet himself describes *The Temple* as "a picture of the many spiritual conflicts that have passed betwixt God and my soul, before I could subject mine to the will of Jesus my master."[17] The individual poems in the collection are titled after acts of worship or the architecture and furnishings of a church or the seasons of the liturgical year or the sacraments or the struggles of the soul. To read *The Temple* is to enter the imaginative world of Herbert and to find ourselves in the sacred space

17. George Herbert, *The Complete English Poems*, ed. John Tobin (London: Penguin Books, 1991), xvi.

of a cavernous soul, a soul that is resonant with the echoes of our own hopes and agonies.

I open *The Temple* and begin with the first and longest poem by Herbert, "The Church-Porch," subtitled "Perirrhanterium." Both titles are significant. "The Church-Porch" suggests that we are at the point of entry. We are on the verge of sacred space. We are about to move into the depths and heights of encountering the holy, the numinous, the divine, the wonder and mystery that flow from the deep dear core of things. The subtitle, "Perirrhanterium," refers to "an instrument for sprinkling holy water, especially upon the newly baptized."[18] Thus the subtitle reinforces that we are at the beginning of a new life in Christ, an impression that is confirmed by the instructional nature of the stanzas that follow.

Near the end of "The Church-Porch," I come across lines that did not register with me as an undergraduate English major nearly fifty years ago:

Resort to sermons, but to prayers most:
Praying's the end of preaching.[19]

The word *end* can be taken simultaneously to mean two different things: the *purpose* of preaching is prayer, and the *conclusion* of preaching is prayer.

Although I have derived my theme from Herbert and although my Beecher predecessors are providing a long-term perspective, I will focus on what it means here and now to claim that "Praying's the end of preaching." The here and now of our own time includes the multiple crises plaguing our global village. Here and now we cling to a spinning

---

18. Herbert, *The Complete English Poems*, 325.
19. Herbert, *The Complete English Poems*, 20.

watered stone whose interconnected systems of life are breaking down. Here and now we have fragmented the human community into groups that are locked in cycles of brutal violence. Here and now different ways of human knowing have splintered into warring modes of perception and cognition that feed the rigid orthodoxies of sectarianism, scientism, and political ideology.

My goal is to show that when "Praying's the end of preaching," prayer is not an escape from the terrifying realities of here and now to a privatized piety, but rather prayer is a different mode of being and doing that engages us with the world in ways that can start and sustain the impulses of transformation.

Henry Ward Beecher holds prayer in as high a place of esteem as Herbert does. Beecher titles one of his major lectures with the single word: "Prayer." In that lecture he states: "I think the most sacred function of the Christian ministry is praying....And it is better than a sermon, it is better than any exhortation. He that knows how to pray for his people, I had almost said, need not trouble himself to preach for them or to them; though that is an exaggeration, of course."[20] I believe that Beecher here comes close in spirit to putting in prose what Herbert expresses in verse:

Resort to sermons, but to prayers most:
Praying's the end of preaching.

At least one subsequent Beecher lecturer strongly shares Beecher's desire to have preachers give more attention to prayer. William Pierson Merrill, who lectured in the academic year 1921–1922, observes:

---

20. Beecher, *Yale Lectures on Preaching*, vol. II, 46–47.

"Protestantism did a great service when it reexalted preaching: but it went off the rails when it did so at the expense of praise and prayer. Preaching will not lose, but gain, when it is seen in proper proportion, and when it is rightly related to other acts, in which worship obtains a more complete expression."[21] "Praying's the end of preaching" is a deceptively simple statement. The matter is much more complex than it sounds. For prayer is a comprehensive, multidimensional phenomenon. As Carol and Philip Zaleski observe in their magisterial volume *Prayer: A History,*

> Traditional spoken and written prayers display a breathtaking variety of forms, including invocation, proclamation, exorcism, novena, meditation, hymn, didactic wisdom, and lament. They may be intricate and lengthy.... Or they may be as short and sharp as a dagger.... They may conjure or abjure, curse or jest, praise or blame, plea or give thanks; they may be joyous, bitter, calm, choleric, charitable, or vindictive; they may burst forth at any hour, under any circumstance, in any place.[22]

As complex and multidimensional as prayer is, there is something elemental about its character, as though it is a reality woven into the very fabric of the world. The Zaleskis write: "When we ask men and women from traditional cultures, those endowed with a lively mythic consciousness, about the origin of prayer, their answers send us back to the beginning of time. Prayer, they tell us, is written into our world primordial charter; it echoes the creator's speech, the animal's lament, the angels' chant."[23]

21. Baxter, *The Heart of the Yale Lectures*, 203; originally appeared in William Pierson Merrill, *The Freedom of the Preacher* (New York: Macmillan, 1922), 45.
22. Philip Zaleski and Carol Zaleski, *Prayer: A History* (Boston: Houghton Mifflin, 2005), 251.
23. Philip Zaleski and Carol Zaleski, *Prayer: A History*, 22.

The Weather of Prayer

The contemporary poet Ellery Akers reveals how we—supposedly sophisticated, postmodern people—may in fact be in touch with the primordial character of prayer through the kind of common experience that Akers probes in her poem "The Word That Is a Prayer":

One thing you know when you say it:
all over the earth people are saying it with you;
a child blurting it out as the seizures take her,
a woman reciting it on a cot in a hospital.
What if you take a cab through the Tenderloin:
at a street light, a man in a wool cap,
yarn unraveling across his face, knocks at the window;
he says, Please.
By the time you hear what he's saying,
the light changes, the cab pulls away,
and you don't go back, though you know
someone just prayed to you the way you pray.
Please: a word so short
it could get lost in the air
as it floats up to God like the feather it is,
knocking and knocking, and finally
falling back to earth as rain
as pellets of ice, soaking a black branch,
collecting in drains, leaching into the ground,
and you walk in that weather every day.[24]

---

24.   Ellery Akers, "The Word That Is a Prayer," *Practicing the Truth*. Copyright © 2015 by Ellery Akers. Reprinted with the permission of The Permissions Company, Inc., on behalf of Autumn House Press, www.autumnhouse.org.

To say that "Preaching's the end of prayer" is to affirm that one of the tasks of preaching is to awaken us to the realization that we walk every day in the weather of prayer. But how is preaching to accomplish this when prayer is itself such a sprawling, varied, multidimensional, primordial reality?

George Herbert provides us with a framework for responding to this question through his metaphor of the temple. Carol and Philip Zaleski reflect on how temples help sustain the praying that goes on in a multitude of places: "We may pray in the bedroom at dawn, in the fields at midday, in the kitchen at dusk. But we are able to pray there because we pray also in a more powerful place, where prayer goes on endlessly, day and night. Prayer does have a wellspring, and its name is the temple."[25]

When Herbert says "Praying's the end of preaching," he has in mind the prayer of the temple, the prayer of the house of worship, the prayer of the church gathered together in holy service. For Herbert the corporate nature of prayer does not domesticate and smooth the ragged edges of what the human heart wants from God. Mark the astounding range of images and phrases that Herbert employs in this sonnet that is one continuous series of appositions for prayer:

> *Prayer the Church's banquet, angel's age,*
> > *God's breath in man returning to his birth,*
> > *The soul in paraphrase, heart in pilgrimage,*
> *The Christian plummet sounding heav'n and earth*
> *Engine against th' Almighty, sinner's tow'r,*
> > *Reversed thunder, Christ-side-piercing spear,*
> > *The six-days world transposing in an hour,*

25. Philip Zaleski and Carol Zaleski, *Prayer: A History,* 241.

> A kind of tune, which all things hear and fear;
> Softness, and peace, and joy, and love, and bliss,
> Exalted manna, gladness of the best,
> Heaven in ordinary, man well drest,
> The milky way, the bird of Paradise,
> Church-bells beyond the stars heard, the soul's blood,
> The land of spices; something understood.[26]

The title of each chapter in this book is drawn directly from Herbert's sonnet. This chapter is titled "The Church's Banquet," the opening phrase the poet uses to describe prayer in his sonnet. If prayer is "the Church's banquet," and if we claim that "Praying's the end of preaching," then that means the purpose of preaching is to invite people to a banquet, a feast, a celebratory meal.

Although Herbert's focus is on corporate prayer, he does appreciate the importance of private personal prayer. Early in "The Church-Porch" he counsels:

> By all means use sometimes to be alone.
> Salute thyself: see what thy soul doth wear.
> Dare to look in thy chest; for 'tis thine own:
> And tumble up and down what thou find'st there.[27]

Some forty stanzas later, however, shortly before Herbert asserts that "Praying's the end of preaching," he observes:

26. Herbert, *The Complete English Poems*, 45–46.
27. Herbert, *The Complete English Poems*, 11, from stanza 25 of "Perirrhanterium."

Though private prayer be a brave design,

Yet public hath more promises, more love:

And love's a weight to hearts, to eyes a sign.

We all are but cold suitors; let us move

Where it is warmest. Leave thy six and seven;

Pray with the most: for where most pray, is heaven.[28]

Thus, when Herbert says "Praying's the end of preaching," he means the corporate prayer of the community of faith: "the Church's banquet."

I believe the poet's counsel about the prayer of the community would strengthen a lot of the preaching. With notable exceptions, the majority of preaching I have heard over the last forty-six years focused more on the individual than the gathered body of Christ. Herbert calls us out of our isolation to join with one another:

We all are but cold suitors; let us move

Where it is warmest. Leave thy six and seven;

Pray with the most: for where most pray, is heaven.

The Unlimited Repertoire of Prayer

Although the "public" prayer of our houses of worship is highly varied, it tends to fall into recognizable patterns that reach across many

---

28. Herbert, *The Complete English Poems*, 19, stanza 67. "Six and seven" is originally a dicing term that came to mean "indifference to the consequence of your action." From the endnotes, 330.

traditions, no matter how much the style and form of their services may differ. I am thinking of six classic kinds of corporate prayer, each of them expressing a different dimension in the divine/human relationship, and each of them manifest in one way or another in a wide range of worship practices:

- Adoration
- Confession
- Supplication
- Intercession
- Thanksgiving
- Lament

To say "Praying's the end of preaching" is to say: Adoration is the end of preaching. Confession is the end of preaching. Supplication is the end of preaching. Intercession is the end of preaching. Thanksgiving is the end of preaching. Lament is the end of preaching. In drawing this implication from Herbert's assertion, I am not claiming that this was the poet's intention. Rather I am using Herbert's poetry to fuel my own work of imaginative homiletical theology.

The six categories of prayer I have named obviously do not exhaust all the forms that prayer may take, but they are comprehensive enough to provide insight into the sprawling, complex, multidimensional, primordial phenomenon of prayer. I will use these six forms of prayer to symbolize and explore the virtually unlimited repertoire of prayer. My aim is to illuminate the theological implications and homiletical possibilities that open up when "Praying's the end of preaching."

Since prayer, whatever form it takes, cultivates a living relationship to God, Herbert's statement means that the end of preaching is the vitalizing, the nurturing, the enriching, the deepening, the broadening, the heightening of our relationship to God.

If the end of preaching is prayer, the richness of prayer, the fullness of prayer, the complexity of prayer, the multidimensionality of prayer, the primordial character of prayer, then a question every preacher and every listener to sermons needs to ask is, what kind of prayer is awakened by the sermons I preach or hear?

I am NOT saying every sermon ought to be about prayer nor that every sermon will conclude with the preacher offering a prayer. Rather I am asking, what kind of living relationship to God does preaching nurture over time? Is it only the relationship of the individual to God? Or does our preaching strengthen the communal relationship between God and the gathered people of God? Does it welcome people to "the Church's banquet"?

Herbert's assertion that "Praying's the end of preaching" carries implicitly within it a standard of critical judgment: namely, does our preaching nurture a rich relationship to God, a relationship in which people move through a broad range of prayer that is extravagant enough to include at the very least adoration, confession, supplication, intercession, thanksgiving, and lament?

It is possible for preaching to encourage and reinforce only one kind of prayer—and to do so sermon after sermon after sermon. I think of a woman who told me of the preacher she listened to while growing up. After every sermon, she always felt the same prayer rising in her heart: "I need to confess my sins to God." It is not wrong for some sermons to lead to confession. Later we will consider how confession is an essential and appropriate end for preaching. But for *all* sermons to lead to confession is to constrict the wholeness of God and to limit the fullness of our relationship to God.

Take a minute to consider the preaching you have received or the preaching you have done. Has that preaching led to a broad repertoire of prayer and a rich relationship to God, or has it reinforced a narrow range of prayer and therefore a diminished relationship to God?

Nothing Is Too Rich to Clothe the Sun

If the end of preaching is prayer then surely sometimes preaching ought to end in adoration. I think of traditional ascriptions of praise to God:

> *Blessing and glory and wisdom*
> *and thanksgiving and honor*
> *and power and might*
> *be to our God forever and ever! Amen. (Revelation 7:12)*

> *Joyful, joyful, we adore thee,*
> *God of glory, Lord of love;*
> *hearts unfold like flowers before thee,*
> *opening to the sun above.*[29]

The adoration of God changes nothing. The adoration of God changes everything. If you judge the adoration of God by utilitarian standards, then it changes nothing. The adoration of God does not turn a profit or plant a field or build a house. The adoration of God has no results that

---

29. "Joyful, Joyful, We Adore Thee," *The United Methodist Hymnal* (Nashville: The United Methodist Publishing House, 1989), no. 89.

you can immediately calculate and quantify, and it is precisely these qualities that make adoration so baffling and so essential in our age. As Leon Wiseltier has argued:

> Quantification is the most overwhelming influence upon the contemporary understanding of, well, everything. It is enabled by the idolatry of data, which has itself been enabled by the almost unimaginable data-generating capabilities of the new technology.
>
> The distinction between knowledge and information is a thing of the past....Such transformations embolden certain high priests in the church of tech to espouse the doctrine of "transhumanism" and to suggest...that our computational ability will carry us magnificently beyond our humanity.[30]

To say in an age of the "idolatry of data" that the adoration of God is the end of preaching is to make clear that one of the purposes of preaching is to keep human consciousness open to those dimensions of reality that are not quantifiable: the numinous, the holy, wonder, wisdom, mystery, awe. When these qualities come alive in the human heart and mind, then it is no longer true that the adoration of God changes nothing. Rather, the adoration of God changes everything. For when we give ourselves utterly and completely to the adoration of God, nothing in creation ever looks the same as it did before. All that *is* becomes charged with meaning. That is why the psalmist's exhortation to praise God flows seamlessly from inanimate natural phenomena to creatures to human beings of every class, gender, and age:

> *Praise the LORD from the earth,*
>
> > *you sea monsters and all deeps,*
>
> *fire and hail, snow and frost,*
>
> > *stormy wind fulfilling his command!*

---

30. Leon Wieseltier, "Among the Disrupted," *NY Times Book Review* (January 18, 2015): 1.

Mountains and all hills,
> *fruit trees and all cedars!*
Wild animals and all cattle,
> *creeping things and flying birds!*

Kings of the earth and all peoples,
> *princes and all rulers of the earth!*
Young men and women alike,
> *old and young together! (Psalm 148:7-12)*

Take note that "creeping things and flying birds" precede "Kings of the earth and all peoples." Snakes and worms, hawks and sparrows come before human potentates! The adoration of God inverts the perceptual hierarchies of human ranking. To adore God is to participate in a process that hums through the whole of creation. To adore God reveals that our overblown estimate of human status is a distortion that feeds our disregard for the ecological web and all the other creatures who are as dependent upon it as we are. According to the psalmist, the creatures have a role in the adoration of God that is every bit as significant as ours. And not just the creatures! But physical phenomena as well:

Fire and hail, snow and frost,
> *stormy wind fulfilling his command!*

Mountains and all hills,
> *fruit trees and all cedars!*

Here are two stanzas from a hymn that draws the insight of the psalmist and the theology of Herbert closer to our scientific ethos:

Have you not known? Have you not heard?

that from the very start

God is the one whose spirit stirred

each atom, star and heart

From God they draw their energy

to spin and burn and beat

and learn the choreography

of matter, light and heat.

God, since each atom, star and heart

depend and wait on you

and on the powers you impart

and constantly renew,

their being is a form of prayer

that makes of time and space

a temple brimming with your care

where all exist by grace.[31]

"Praying's the end of preaching" means that one of the purposes of preaching is to remind us that the materiality of existence is a freely bestowed gift that we did nothing to initiate or attain. When we realize

---

31. Thomas H. Troeger, "Have you not known? Have you not heard?" *God, you made all things for singing: Hymn texts, anthems, and poems for a new millennium* (New York and Oxford: Oxford University Press, 2009), 29.

this in the marrow of our bones, no expression of adoration seems too extravagant.

George Herbert knew the impulse to extravagance in the adoration of God. In his poem "Jordan (2)," he reflects that when he first started writing "of heav'nly joys"

Nothing could seem too rich to clothe the sun.[32]

The word *sun* here is a pun on "son," as in "son of God." In Herbert's day that pun was one of the conventions of religious verse.

Herbert's vivid line—"Nothing could seem too rich to clothe the sun!"—expresses the character of extravagant language that marked not only the poet's early poetic idiom but also the development of prayers of adoration in many early liturgies of the church. Robert J. Ledogar, who has written a study of praise verbs in early Greek *anaphora*, observes that "instead of a single word for praise, there is a string of synonymous infinitives which seem to express by their very multiplicity the inability of human language to praise God adequately, and at the same time the insistent need to do so."[33] Ledogar traces this tradition back to

the famous *Kaddish* of the Jewish prayer-book. This was the Aramaic "doxology" with which a teacher or preacher ends his discourse, and with which every major portion of the synagogue service is brought to an end.... "Blessed, praised and glorified, exalted, extolled and honored, magnified and lauded be the Name of the Holy one, blessed be he; though he be above all the blessings and hymns, praises and consolation, which are uttered in the world; and say ye Amen."[34]

32. Herbert, *The Complete English Poems*, 94.
33. Robert J. Ledogar, *Acknowledgment: Praise-Verbs in the Early Greek Anaphora* (Rome: Casa Editrice Herder, 1968), 1.
34. Ledogar, *Acknowledgment: Praise-Verbs in the Early Greek Anaphora*, 48.

To say that "Praying's the end of preaching" is to remind us preachers that we are using language to help people acknowledge "the inability of human language to praise God adequately, and at the same time the insistent need to do so."

"Praying's the end of preaching." Therefore, the end of preaching includes the adoration of God, bringing people to that liminal domain where they join "the Church's banquet" and feel and think in their hearts and minds that nothing—nothing!—is "too rich to clothe the sun."

Chapter Two

"The Soul in Paraphrase, Heart in Pilgrimage"

Having examined why sermons need to awaken the adoration of God, we turn to consider how confession, supplication, intercession, thanksgiving, and lament amplify the meaning of George Herbert's claim that "Praying's the end of preaching." Our exploration of this broad repertoire of prayer is guided by Herbert's description of prayer as "The soul in paraphrase, heart in pilgrimage."

Think of those times when someone asked you to paraphrase something they did not understand, to restate some complex matter in a way that they could follow and comprehend. It is often not easy to paraphrase something, especially if the first way you put the matter reflects exactly how you think about it.

The Recovery of Soul

If it is difficult to paraphrase language, how would you paraphrase something as elusive and complex as the human soul? The task is even more challenging for us than in Herbert's day because, as Edward Hirsch has observed, "we have almost lost the word *soul* as a figure of deep spiritual essence.... When we lose a word we also lose its meaning. The depletion in our vocabulary leads to a dire loss of soulfulness."[1]

Preaching whose end is prayer can help us recover soul and a life marked by soulfulness. By *soul*, I do not mean an ephemeral ghost that inhabits the body and flies away at death. Rather I mean the human creature in its totality before God, the sum of our being that is more than the aggregate of our individual characteristics. I mean the core identity that reminds us that, in the words of Marilynne Robinson, "human beings are invested with a degree of value that we can't honor appropriately. An overabundance that is magical."[2]

The medieval mystic Meister Eckhart (1260–1328) gives expression to that "overabundance that is magical" when he writes:

> What God is doing in the core of my soul is hidden from me and that is of great benefit. Since the soul does not know, it wonders, and wondering, it seeks. For the soul knows very well that something's afoot, even though it does not know what or how. As long as what it is doing in the core of my soul is concealed, I am always after it.... It appears and disappears, I plead and sigh for it.[3]

1. Edward Hirsch, *How to Read a Poem and Fall in Love with Poetry* (San Diego: Harcourt, 1999), 257.

2. As quoted by Wyatt Mason, "Saying Grace: The Revelations of Marilynne Robinson," *New York Times Magazine* (October 5, 2014): 27.

3. A bulletin from Bethany House of Prayer in Arlington, Massachusetts. Information is available at www.BethanyHouseArlington.org.

When "Praying is the end of preaching," then preaching nurtures "the soul in paraphrase," nurtures our insight into the depths of our humanity, into the something that's "afoot" in the core of our being. That insight includes a heightened awareness of what Herbert calls the "heart in pilgrimage." The phrase "heart in pilgrimage" comes in Herbert's sonnet directly after "The soul in paraphrase." They are in the same poetic line, separated only by a comma, suggesting that the second phrase is an apposition to the first. How do we paraphrase a soul? We study the "heart in pilgrimage," and all the domains through which it travels when we offer to God the full repertoire of prayer. We discover that the soul often travels from rhapsodic praise to regions of remorse and sorrow. The wonder and astonishment that accompany the adoration of God can send the "heart in pilgrimage" to confession.

> *Holy, holy, holy is the* LORD *of hosts;*
> *the whole earth is full of his glory.* . . .
>
> Woe is me! I am lost, for I am a man of unclean lips, and I live among
> a people of unclean lips; yet my eyes have seen the King, the LORD of
> hosts! (Isaiah 6:3, 5)

Those beloved, familiar lines reveal one of the most traveled routes of the "heart in pilgrimage." Astonished by the glory of God, we become aware of how fragmented and contentious we are, both as individuals and as a community. When "Praying's the end of preaching," one of the prayers it nurtures is the prayer of confession and repentance.

The Necessity of Confession in a Feel-Good Culture

In a feel-good culture, however, the call to confession often meets resistance. I think of people who have told me that the very idea of confession makes them feel bad about themselves, so they refuse to do it. As a woman once said to me: "At the prayer of confession I just sit with my arms crossed and my lips shut." In some cases this resistance flows from understandable causes. Many people have suffered under a form of Christianity that concentrates unremittingly on sin and the cultivation of guilt. Resisting this distortion of Christian faith is a sign of spiritual health: People are rightly fighting back against oppressive religion.

In other cases, people resist confession because sin has been narrowly defined as hubris, as pride and arrogance. This narrow definition of sin does not allow for those whose sin is not pride. As Elisabeth Schüssler Fiorenza has pointed out, some people's sin is not arrogance but a failure to affirm their self-worth and use the gifts God has given them.[4]

In short, there are often good reasons people resist prayers of confession, including an unremitting focus upon sin, the inculcation of guilt, and a definition of sin that is incongruent with their life situation.

But having allowed for those good reasons, we need to acknowledge the self-deception that often feeds our resistance to confession. The corrective to the distortions that people rightly reject is not the abandonment of confession but a healthy reframing of the act. This is exactly what Neil Pembroke attempts to do in his book *Pastoral Care in Worship: Liturgy and Psychology in Dialogue.* Pembroke writes that "forgiveness of

---

4. Elisabeth Schüssler Fiorenza, *Bread Not Stone: The Challenge of Feminist Biblical Interpretation* (Boston: Beacon Press, 1984), xv.

sin needs to be seen as the means to the end of restoring a broken rela-tionship with God. It is communion with God that is the true aim and destiny of humankind."[5]

Pembroke observes that the reformer Ulrich Zwingli (1484–1531) realized how tangled the human soul is about sin and confession. Zwingli so organized his service of worship that confession was literally the end of preaching.

> The notion of Christ as mirror is behind Zwingli's pattern of placing the prayer of confession after the sermon. He seems to have had in mind the notion that we can only truly confess our sins after our true nature has been illumined by the Word. An effective proclamation of the Word has the power to open eyes and ears, hearts and minds. Hiding is more difficult when the spotlight of truth shines in one's direction. Game-playing and pettiness is shown up in the light of the Gospel.[6]

Such theological insight into our game-playing and pettiness reminds us that there is a kind of feeling bad about ourselves, a kind of guilt that is appropriate and healthy. Wislawa Szymborska, winner of the Nobel Prize for Literature in 1996, expresses this with wit and wisdom. Born in Poland in 1923, Szymborska knew firsthand the terror and brutality of the twentieth century. Her poem "In Praise of Feeling Bad about Your-self" helps us understand why confession is essential:

> *The buzzard never says it is to blame.*
>
> *The panther wouldn't know what scruples mean.*
>
> *When the piranha strikes, it feels no shame.*

---

5. Neil Pembroke, *Pastoral Care in Worship: Liturgy and Psychology in Dialogue* (London: T & T Clark International, 2010), 7.
6. Neil Pembroke, *Pastoral Care in Worship*, 21.

If snakes had hands, they'd claim their hands were clean.

A jackal doesn't understand remorse.
Lions and lice don't waver in their course.
Why should they, when they know they're right?

Though hearts of killer whales may weigh a ton,
in every other way they're light.

On this third planet of the sun
among the signs of bestiality
a clear conscience is Number One.[7]

Feeling badly about ourselves is not always a bad response to those things that we have done and to those things that we have left undone. To say that "Praying's the end of preaching" means that the end of preaching includes confession. Preachers, therefore, are faced with the complex task of disentangling confession from its distortions, so they can witness to its healthy, restorative possibilities for us as individuals as well as a society. Without confession, the paraphrase of the soul is incomplete and distorted, and the "heart in pilgrimage" will never reach its ultimate destination. If we affirm faith in a God of justice and compassion, and if in the presence of that God we look honestly at ourselves, then we will confess that we have not loved God with our whole heart and we have not loved our neighbors as ourselves.

We are truly sorry and we humbly repent.

In 2016, on the day following the national celebration of Martin Luther King Jr., I was reminded once again how essential it is that the

---

7. Wislawa Szymborska, *Poems New and Collected* (San Diego: Harcourt, 1998), 168.

end of preaching includes confession, includes the acknowledgment of hard-to-face truth about ourselves and our society, things we would rather hide from. A front-page article in the *Portland Herald* featured the Reverend Kenneth Lewis, who said: "The most powerful thing anyone can do to fight racism is to identify it, whether within themselves or others.... 'Calling it what it is starts the process of dealing with it.'"[8] That to me is a concise, healthy, contemporary definition of confession. Confession is not an end in itself but rather a realization that starts a process, beckoning the "heart in pilgrimage" to keep traveling. To confess our sins to God is to come to terms with who we really are, to know more completely and more accurately "The soul in paraphrase":

Creator of all that is
we are not
what you made us to be.

If our sin is pride
remind us
every breath
is a gift from you.

If our sin is humility
remind us
we are made
in your image.

---

8. Kelley Bouchard, "Pursuing King's 'Beloved Community,'" *Portland Herald* (January 18, 2016): A6. Lewis is pastor of Green Memorial AME Zion Church in Portland, Maine.

If our sin is the neglect of our souls

remind us

you are praying

through our sighs

too deep for words.

If our sin is neglect of others

remind us

Christ speaks

through cries of human need.

Whatever our sin

remind us

your mercy is endless

for those who love you,

and we can be a new creation

through Jesus Christ. AMEN.[9]

Overcoming Ambivalence about Praying for Ourselves

"Praying's the end of preaching." Therefore, adoration is the end of preaching, confession is the end of preaching. And sometimes supplication is the end of preaching. Supplication is praying for ourselves, asking God for what we need. At one level, it sounds simple, easy, direct. The

9. Thomas H. Troeger, *Borrowed Light: Hymn texts, prayers, and poems* (New York: Oxford University Press, 1994), 127.

Zaleskis, whose history of prayer I have cited earlier, believe that the prayer of supplication may go back to the origins of human language: "Nothing is more basic than a call for help. It seems likely that the very word *help*—perhaps the first word coined by our hominid ancestors—appears in more prayers than any other, outpacing *save* and *bless*."[10] Yet as simple and direct as the word *help* may appear, there is ambivalence in the human soul about asking God for help. Can it be that the mysterious, wondrous, magnificent God whom we adore would actually attend to us finite creatures who live on this tiny mote of dust in the vast immensities of space? We pick up a hint of that ambivalence in the prayer that King Solomon offers at the dedication of the temple. Early in the prayer, Solomon wonders: "'But will God indeed dwell on the earth? Even heaven and the highest heaven cannot contain you, much less this house that I have built!'" (1 Kings 8:27). Yet in the very next verse, Solomon proceeds boldly to ask God's help: "'Regard your servant's prayer and his plea, O LORD my God, . . . that your servant prays to you today'" (1 Kings 8:28). Solomon then follows his general supplication with twenty-two verses of the specific prayers that he wants God to answer, petitions that include a vast range of human predicaments, from sin to drought and famine and war. Solomon clearly does not allow his awe for God to restrain his supplications for divine help.

But for many human souls, prayers of supplication may be as problematic as prayers of confession. I have never forgotten a particular response to a sermon that I preached years ago. A woman came up to me and said: "I have always been able to pray for others. Every day I pray for people who I know are in deep need. But I have never been able to pray for myself. I thought I was being too selfish if I prayed for what I need.

---

10. Philip Zaleski and Carol Zaleski, *Prayer: A History* (Boston: Houghton Mifflin, 2005), 97.

But today through your sermon, I heard Christ saying: 'Pray for yourself. Bring your need to me.'" The woman was standing in a line of worshippers at a conference, and there were scores of others waiting to shake my hand. She quickly disappeared in the sea of people.

I never saw the woman again, but her words have often returned to haunt me as a preacher. What kind of preaching and Christian nurture had the woman received that would lead her to this state of soul: "I have never been able to pray for myself. I thought I was being too selfish to pray for me"? Her words make me think of many other people who have asked me, "Do you think it's all right for me to pray for this?" Why all these worries and rules about prayer, especially when we pray for ourselves? What holds us back from being as extravagant as King Solomon in his petitions?

There are some good reasons people hesitate to pray for themselves. They do not want to reduce their spiritual life to narcissism. Most people have enough self-awareness that they want to avoid contracting the world down to their personal concerns.

As valid as these cautions may be, I am struck with how Jesus does not fence prayer in with rubrics and protocols. Instead, Jesus simply urges us to get started: "'Ask, and it will be given you; search, and you will find; knock, and the door will be opened for you'" (Matthew 7:7). Ask. Seek. Knock. Get to it. Start now. Begin praying. Do not worry if your prayer is right or wrong.

When Jesus says "ask," he does not specify what we will receive. When he says "seek," he does not predict what we will find. When he says "knock," he does not describe what the open door will disclose. The important thing is to dare to pray for ourselves.

"Praying's the end of preaching." Therefore, at least sometimes, the end of preaching is supplication, unreservedly asking God for what we need. What about the preaching you do or hear? Does it at least sometimes nurture supplication? Without supplication, "The soul in paraphrase" will be incomplete and distorted.

The Inter-Connective Tissue of Our Common Creaturehood

I believe that if the woman who said to me, "I have never been able to pray for myself," did begin to pray for herself, it would enrich her prayer for others. Christ says, "Love your neighbor *as yourself.*" Clearly there is a kind of love of self that is healthy and right. Such love puts us in touch with our humanity, with our elemental needs, with our own brokenness and fears, with our deepest questions and struggles, and our highest hopes and dreams. To pray for ourselves out of these profound realities is part of finding our connection to other human beings. Praying for ourselves instructs us in the way of praying for others. For if we are to love our neighbors as we love ourselves, then we are to pray for others as we pray for ourselves.

I recall a particular time when someone prayed for me and sent me a letter about her prayer on my behalf. It was a time in my life when I was struggling with a grave and difficult decision. The person who wrote me began by outlining what she knew of the decision, the conflicting forces and factors that pulled me in one direction and then the other. Her description and analysis were accurate. They fit the contours of my thought and feeling. Then having identified my dilemma, the woman wrote: "I know when I have faced such a decision I did not want

someone to tell me, 'This is what you must do, this is how you must decide.' Instead, I have asked for myself the guidance of the Spirit. And so
that is what I am praying for you: for the guidance of the Spirit."

The clarity of the woman's prayer and the way it arose out of the
depths of her own prayers for herself, reached directly to my own need
and empowered me to pray for the guidance of the Spirit. I found myself
becoming more attentive to perspectives that had been blocked from
view by my fixation on a particular way of perceiving the situation. And
in time I was able to decide wisely.

The beauty of the woman's prayer is that she did not displace God
with herself and with her own wishes for me. Her prayer flowed from
the integrity of her own soul and what she had learned about prayer by
praying for herself.

The process can also work in reverse: in praying for others we learn
to pray more faithfully for ourselves because compassion for the other
awakens a sense of our common humanity. We discover that there are
resonances between another soul in paraphrase and our soul in paraphrase, points of conjunction between another heart in pilgrimage and
our heart in pilgrimage. The Zaleskis offer a term for understanding this
phenomenon that they draw from the work of Charles Williams, who

> believed that intercessory prayer was the sovereign remedy for the sinful
> will to power. He loved to meditate on the mystery of human creatures
> bearing one another's burdens in prayer, "dying in each other's life, liv-
> ing in each other's death." "Co-inherence" he called this mystery, bor-
> rowing the word used in Christian dogma for the mutual indwelling
> of the three Persons of the Trinity. Human beings are social animals,
> Williams observed, and in bearing one another's burden in prayer we
> foreshadow the ideal commonwealth, the new Jerusalem.[11]

11. Philip Zaleski and Carol Zaleski, *Prayer: A History*, 86–87.

Williams's principle of co-inherence is manifest in Jesus's command: "'Love your enemies and pray for those who persecute you'" (Matthew 5:44). It is significant that this command is one continuous sentence: "'Love your enemies and pray for those who persecute you.'" If the command read only "Love your enemies," then the command would not point us to the source of grace who can transform how we look at our enemies. Praying for those who persecute us opens us to a different perception of those from whom we are alienated. When we pray for those who persecute us, the category "enemy" begins to dissolve in the waters of the Spirit, revealing the essential humanness of the other, a humanness that we share in common.

Praying for our enemies reveals in an especially dramatic way the dynamic interaction between praying for ourselves and praying for others. When we pray for those who "are in trouble, sorrow, need, sickness, or any other adversity," then we open ourselves to the inter-connective tissue of the common creaturehood that we share with the whole human family and with the entire ecosystem. For now, in light of the ecological crisis, it is no longer adequate to limit co-inherence to the human family and to the foreshadowing of "the ideal commonwealth, the new Jerusalem." We must expand our intercession, our co-inherence, to all the elements, processes, and creatures of earth whose existence we human beings have put at risk. Thomas Berry succinctly states the principle this way: "While we have recognized the inseparable nature of communion of God with the human community, we have not yet realized that this communion, to be perfect, must include communion with Earth."[12]

---

12. Thomas Berry, *The Christian Future and the Fate of Earth* (Maryknoll, NY: Orbis Books, 2009), 11.

If "Praying's the end of preaching," and praying includes intercession, then intercession in a time of global ecological breakdown needs
to include intercession for the elements, processes, and creatures of the
entire planet. Such an inclusive cosmic understanding of intercessory
prayer marks the ministry of two religious leaders in New England, Steve
Blackmer and Norman MacLeod, who are working to engage the re-
sources of faith to address the crisis of the ecosphere. They hired me as
the preacher for a series of services of worship calling us to ecologically
responsible living. Although I was the preacher, they laid out the con-
cepts and vision that shaped my sermons, and they worked with me in
planning the liturgies.

Blackmer and MacLeod proposed that we use a traditional pattern
of Holy Week worship to give shape to our sequence of services. But instead of only rehearsing the Passion of Jesus in Jerusalem, we focused on
how the cosmic Christ is suffering through our abuse of the biosphere.
The services were held in New Hampshire and Vermont over the course
of several days, in churches and chapels, in deep woods, and on the
northern banks of the Connecticut River.

At one point in my preparations, I was reading Elizabeth Kolbert's
The Sixth Extinction: An Unnatural History. I read there a list of endan-
gered sea creatures and found myself moved to offer a prayer that, in a
modified form, later found its way into one of the services:

O Creator of all that is,
protect and preserve:
"Tiger sharks, lemon sharks,
gray reef sharks, blue-spine unicorn fish,
yellow boxfish, spotted boxfish,

conspicuous angelfish,

Barrier Reef anemonefish,

Barrier Reef chromis, minifin parrotfish,

Pacific long nose parrotfish,

somber sweetlips, four spot herring,

yellow fin tuna, common dolphinfish,

deceiver fangblenny, yellow spotted sawtail,

barred rabbitfish, blunt-headed wrasse,

and striped cleaner wrasse."[13]

In Christ's name, AMEN.

Accustomed to an idiom that is primarily focused on God and human beings we may at first find that such a prayer rings strangely upon our ears. But the prayer is congruent with the cosmological dimensions of the *logos* as we find them in the prologue to John and the Christ hymn in Colossians.

These biblical passages also shaped the call to worship in one of our ecological liturgies based upon the passion of the cosmic Christ:

We gather in the name of the Word

through whom all things came into being

and without whom

not one thing came into being.

We gather in the name of the one

in whom all things in the heavens

and here on planet Earth

---

13. Elizabeth Kolbert, *The Sixth Extinction: An Unnatural History* (New York: Henry Holt and Company, 2014), 139.

were created,

things visible and invisible.

We gather in the name of the cosmic Christ,

the one in whom all things hold together,

the one who spoke seven last words

from the cross,

the one whose sad and pained voice

we hear speaking now

through the cries of planet Earth.

In that same service, the congregation read Psalm 104, which observes:

O LORD, how manifold are your works!

   In wisdom you have made them all;

   the earth is full of your creatures.

Yonder is the sea, great and wide,

   creeping things innumerable are there,

   living things both small and great. (Psalm 104:24-25)

including,

somber sweetlips, four spot herring,

yellow fin tuna, common dolphinfish,

deceiver fangblenny.

To say in our time and place "Praying's the end of preaching" means that preaching should give us a sense of co-inherence with God's suffering planet Earth. Some might protest that praying's not adequate. We don't need prayer; we need action. Although there is always the possibility that people will not live what they pray, we need to remember that prayer also has the power to incite and sustain action. George Herbert gave witness to the dynamic interconnection between prayers of intercession and action, how one empowers the other: "If I be bound to pray for all that be in distress, I am sure that I am bound so far as it is in my power to practice what I pray for. And though I do not wish for the like occasion every day, yet let me tell you, I would not willingly pass one day of my life without comforting a sad soul, or shewing mercy; and I praise God for this opportunity."[14]

To say "Praying's the end of preaching" means that the end of preaching is intercession—intercession through prayer and action as one interfused reality, each sustaining and deepening the other. Without intercession the "heart in pilgrimage" only travels in its home territory.

What about the preaching you do or hear? Does it sometimes end in intercession? Does it increase our sense of co-inherence with the whole creaturely family of God's suffering planet Earth?

Overcoming the Reluctance to Give Thanks

Intercession as well as confession and supplication involve asking God for something, either for ourselves or others. As essential as all three are to a vital prayer life, a healthy relationship, including our relationship to God, always involves giving as well as receiving, and finding the balance between receiving and giving is often difficult for us human creatures. For

---

14. Philip Zaleski and Carol Zaleski, *Prayer: A History*, 349. Italics are in the quotation as printed by the Zaleskis. The quotation originally appears in Izaak Walton, *The Life of Mr. George Herbert* (Tho. Newcomb, 1670).

nearly forty years I have had the privilege of guest preaching in congregations throughout North America. During that time I have participated in a form of corporate prayer that has become common to a great many different traditions. The order of service often calls it "joys and concerns." Sometimes, the joys and concerns have been collected ahead of time on a tablet of paper or people will speak them aloud prior to praying, and the minister or priest writes them down and then offers prayers, or the person leading the prayer will offer a petition and then allow a period of time when people may pray their concerns aloud or in silence.

No matter what form these prayers take, no matter what the tradition or denomination, I have observed the following pattern to be nearly universally true: When it comes to concerns and prayers for others, the church fills with the sound of the names of particular persons and places and needs. But when it comes time to offer prayers of thanksgiving, silence often descends. There are a few voices here and there—"Thank you for the lovely day," "Thank you for the children's choir"—but the prayer of thanksgiving seldom rises to the level of the chorus of human need. Why does "The soul in paraphrase, the heart in pilgrimage" find it so hard to travel to the land of gratitude? Why be stingy with thanks?

I think what is involved in learning to thank God is the same pattern we observe in children learning to say thanks. They do not do it automatically. We have to teach them. How many times were you told as a child, "Say, 'thank you'"? How many times, if you are a parent, did you say to your own children, "Say, 'thank you'"? However, when we become adults, I believe it takes something more sophisticated than our early childhood instruction.

Becoming an adult involves gaining a sense of autonomy and self-achievement, characteristics that can block our awareness of how dependent we are upon the source of every good and perfect gift. There-fore, our preaching needs to lead to the recovery of gratitude by breaking through the illusion of self-sufficiency.

Making this breakthrough has been complicated by the way the term *gratitude* has been hijacked by the self-improvement movement. In an article with the intriguing title "The Selfish Side of Gratitude," Barbara Ehrenreich reports:

> Writers in *Time* magazine, *The New York Times* and *Scientific American* recommended [gratitude] as a surefire ticket to happiness and even bet-ter health. Robert Emmons, a psychology professor at the University of California, Davis, who studies the "science of gratitude," argues that it leads to a stronger immune system and lower blood pressure, as well as "more joy and pleasure."…It's possible to achieve the recommended levels of gratitude without spending a penny or uttering a word. All you have to do is to generate, within yourself, the good feelings associated with gratitude, and then bask in its warm, comforting glow. If there is any loving involved in this, it is self-love, and the current hoopla around gratitude is a celebration of onanism.[15]

Gratitude focused on strengthening the immune system, lowering blood pressure, and generating good feelings within oneself is something com-pletely different from the gratitude that the prayer of great thanksgiving urges: "It is right, and a good and joyful thing, always and everywhere to give thanks to you, Father/Mother Almighty, Creator of heaven and earth." Such gratitude is based not upon how well life is going but upon the recognition that we did absolutely nothing to bring ourselves into existence, that every breath is borrowed air, that to live is to receive and to answer back, always and everywhere: thank you, Lord, thank you.

15. Barbara Ehrenreich, "The Selfish Side of Gratitude," *The New York Times*, Sunday Review (January 3, 2016): 3.

Henry Ward Beecher in his second series of lectures spoke about the robust, resilient character of biblical gratitude: "You will be struck, if you look through your concordance of the New Testament, to see how much thanksgiving is insisted upon. Now, by thanksgiving I do not understand a cold 'thank you.' I understand by it an exultant state of mind,—cheerful, hopeful, loving, yearning, upspringing, all running in the direction of joy and gratitude and praise."[16]

The human heart does not automatically beat with such thanksgiving. As George Herbert observes in his poetic prayer "Gratefulness," no matter how extravagant God's gifts are, the heart is always asking for more and more. Instead of thanksgiving, there is an insatiable greed that fuels "Perpetual knockings at [God's] door." In the concluding stanza the poet asks for a heart that is

> *Not thankful, when it pleaseth me;*
> *As if thy blessings had spare days:*
> *But such a heart, whose pulse may be*
> *Thy praise.*[17]

Sometimes literalism kills the meaning of a poem, but sometimes it can plant the meaning in our very cells. Take your pulse. Right now: find your pulse. And then with every pulse beat, say aloud, "Thank you, God, thank you, God, thank you, God."

"The soul in paraphrase" can include the beat of our pulse, and the "heart in pilgrimage" can include the valved muscle pumping blood through our body. O Lord, we ask for the same heart that the poet seeks:

---

16. Henry Ward Beecher, *Yale Lectures on Preaching*, three volumes in one (New York: Fords, Howard, & Hulbert, 1892), vol. II, 144.

17. George Herbert, *The Complete English Poems*, ed. John Tobin (London: Penguin Books, 1991), 115–16.

Not thankful, when it pleaseth me;
As if thy blessings had spare days:
But such a heart, whose pulse may be
    Thy praise.

This is the posture of soul, the generosity of spirit, the inclination of consciousness that is nurtured when "Praying's the end of preaching" and praying includes thanksgiving.

What about the preaching you do or hear? Does it at least sometimes end in thanksgiving? Does it increase our capacity to give thanks to God always and everywhere?

Offering Lament Instead of Theological Snake Oil

When we read the Psalms we discover giving thanks does not preclude the expression of sorrow. The Book of Psalms that ends "Let everything that lives praise the Lord!" also contains some of the most anguished prayers of lament ever uttered:

How long, O LORD? Will you forget me forever?
    How long will you hide your face from me? (Psalm 13:1)

My God, my God, why have you forsaken me?
    Why are you so far from helping me, from the words of my
    groaning?
O my God, I cry by day, but you do not answer;
    and by night, but find no rest. (Psalm 22:1-2)

Lament is as essential as any other form of prayer I have named. Prayers of lament allow us to express our anger, our sorrow, our perplexity and desperation in the face of tragedy. Without lament, "The soul in paraphrase" is impartial and distorted, and the "heart in pilgrimage" is forced to carry a burden that goes unacknowledged.

To understand the importance of lament, think of what it is like when you are in mourning or sadness or a time of doubt and struggle. Whom do you most want to be with you? I will speak for myself. I do not want those people who will offer me theological snake oil. I do not want people who will attempt to sweep aside my sadness or my anger with theological explanations of such thin substance that they evaporate as swiftly as they leave the speaker's mouth. Instead I want with me those who have the wisdom to know there is "a time to weep, and a time to laugh; / a time to mourn, and a time to dance" (Ecclesiastes 3:4), and who, when it is time to weep and mourn, do not dismiss my tears by saying that laughter and dancing are just around the corner.

What about the preaching you do or hear? Does it at least sometimes end in lament?

In American culture we often think of lament and praise, sorrow and thanksgiving as polar opposites. This polar opposition sometimes gets translated into congregations who only want sermons and services that are upbeat. They want praise and thanksgiving minus lament. They want joy and peace minus sorrow.

In his book *Pastoral Care in Worship: Liturgy and Psychology in Dialogue*, Neil Pembroke names the serious implications of not providing for lament in our services of worship:

> It doesn't seem to occur to many worship leaders that complaining to
> God and expressing anger have a central place in Christian liturgy. If we

fail, however, to provide people who are experiencing rage, confusion, and anguish with a liturgical expression of what they are feeling, we isolate and alienate them.

They feel cut off and disenfranchised because the message that they get is that their feelings are not acceptable—or at least not acceptable in this place.[18]

George Herbert evidently knew about the need of the soul to rant against God. Just two lines after "The soul in paraphrase, heart in pilgrimage" Herbert turns to the imagery of warfare, describing prayer as an "Engine against th' Almighty." "The soul in paraphrase" includes our fury at the God we thank and praise. In acknowledging this, Herbert continues in his poetry the witness of the Psalms.

Although many congregations may fail to provide for an adequate expression of lament, there is a notable exception to this in the worship of many African American churches. Drawing on their rich traditions of song and prayer, Otis Moss III observes in his Beecher lectures of 2014: "The pain during the week is connected to the sacred service on Sunday. There is no strict line of demarcation between the existential state of a disenfranchised person of color and the sacred disciplines of prayer, worship and service to humanity."[19]

I believe Henry Ward Beecher would be attuned to the spirit of what Moss observes. For Beecher realized that African American spirituals provide a life-giving witness to the necessity and power of lament. In 1871 Beecher welcomed to New York, amidst racist opposition from the daily newspapers, the Fisk Jubilee Singers, who were famous for performing what W. E. B. DuBois calls "The Sorrow Songs," songs that "tell

18. Pembroke, *Pastoral Care in Worship*, 46.
19. Otis Moss III, the Beecher lectures, 2014, as transcribed from the Yale Divinity School video archive.

of death and suffering and unvoiced longing toward a truer world, of misty wanderings and hidden ways."[20]

Without the expression of lament we disconnect our preaching and worship from the raw, fragmented reality of people's lives and fail to provide the pastoral care for which human beings hunger and thirst. We effectively warp "the soul in paraphrase" and put up a barrier to the "heart in pilgrimage." Sermons and services that are entirely upbeat destroy the essential interconnection of lament and praise, sorrow and thanksgiving. They block having a full relationship with God. They damage the soul. Not just the soul of the individual but the soul of a congregation. Dorothy C. McDougall puts it this way: "The danger of ignoring the role that lament can play in authentic worship is that liturgy can result in a schizophrenic indulgence in ecclesial camaraderie removed from the exigencies of real life."[21]

The God whose presence we celebrate is the God whose absence drives us to despair. The God we praise is the God who bears our anger. The God to whom we give thanks is the God who counts our tears and hears our sighs. Instead of being polar opposites lament and praise, sorrow and thanksgiving are part of the inter-connective tissue of our humanity, of the very way God created us and relates to us.

The Psalms frequently intermingle lament and thanksgiving, and W. E. B. DuBois observes there is a similar inter-connective character in the sorrow songs:

> Through all the sorrow of the Sorrow Songs there breathes a hope—a faith in the ultimate justice of things. The minor cadences of despair

---

20. W. E. B. DuBois, "The Sorrow Songs," *The Souls of Black Folk*, as found at http://www.bartleby.com/114/14.html. There is no pagination, but the paragraph is number 6.
21. Dorothy C. McDougall, *The Cosmos as the Primary Sacrament: The Horizon for an Ecological Sacramental Theology* (New York: Peter Lang, 2003), 149.

change often to triumph and calm confidence. Sometimes it is faith in life, sometimes a faith in death, sometimes assurance of boundless justice in some fair world beyond. But whichever it is, the meaning is always clear: that sometime, somewhere, men will judge men by their souls and not by their skins.[22]

When we pray and the waters of the Holy Spirit flow over and through us, then our lament and praise, our sorrow and thanksgiving flow together in the same stream. "Praying's the end of preaching," and praying includes lament.

What about the preaching you do or hear? Does it at least sometimes engage our need to lament? Does it help us release to God our sense of abandonment and our profoundest sorrows?

I end this chapter with a brief story of contemporary lament. Several years ago, one of my best friends, the fine American composer Sally Ann Morris, phoned me in deep sorrow. A wonderful young man she knew had just died of AIDS. Grief gripped Morris completely. She had no words for her sorrow. So instead she composed music expressing her loss. She subsequently sent me the music and a recording of her playing and humming the score, and asked me to provide words of lament.

The sequence of creating the hymn is significant: first was the music, later came the words. Lament may be a sound before it is language. "The soul in paraphrase" may sound as music before it speaks; the "heart in pilgrimage" may find strength for the journey in song. So when we consider the question "Does preaching at least sometimes engage our need to lament?" we need to think about sound as well as language.

Here are the words awakened by Morris's lyric, minor-keyed, musical lament:

22. DuBois, "The Sorrow Songs," paragraph 23.

God weeps with us who weep and mourn,
God's tears flow down with ours,
and God's own heart is bruised and worn
from all the heavy hours
of watching while the soul's bright fire
burned lower day by day,
and pulse and breath and love's desire
dimmed down to ash and clay.

Through tears and sorrow, God, we share
a sense of your vast grief:
the weight of bearing every prayer
for healing and relief,
the burden of our questions why,
the doubts that they engage,
and as our friends and lovers die,
our hopelessness and rage.

And yet because, like us, you weep,
we trust you will receive
and in your tender heart will keep
the ones for whom we grieve
while with your tears our hearts will taste
the deep dear core of things
from which both life and death are graced
by love's renewing springs.[23]

---

23. Thomas H. Troeger, *Above the Moon Earth Rises: Hymn texts, anthems, and poems for a new creation* (New York: Oxford University Press, 2002), 40.

Chapter Three

"Something Understood"

Consider once again the astounding range of images and phrases that Herbert employs in his sonnet that is one continuous series of appositions for prayer:

> *Prayer the Church's banquet, angel's age,*
> *God's breath in man returning to his birth,*
> *The soul in paraphrase, heart in pilgrimage,*
> *The Christian plummet sounding heav'n and earth*
> *Engine against th' Almighty, sinner's tow'r,*
> *Reversed thunder, Christ-side-piercing spear,*
> *The six-days world transposing in an hour,*
> *A kind of tune, which all things hear and fear;*
> *Softness, and peace, and joy, and love, and bliss,*
> *Exalted manna, gladness of the best,*
> *Heaven in ordinary, man well drest,*
> *The milky way, the bird of Paradise,*

Church-bells beyond the stars heard, the soul's blood,
The land of spices; something understood.

Take special note of the last two words: "something understood."

Fully Known and Comprehended by God

Prayer is "something understood," not "something answered." That final word reframes how we look at prayer and what it means to say "Praying's the end of preaching." If the sonnet ended with the word "answered" rather than "understood," then prayer for the poet would be about getting answers, and the purpose of preaching would be to set people praying in order for them to have God answer them. God would be reduced to an answer man, an answer woman. But if prayer is something understood, then preaching and praying are less about answers and more about the truth that the full range of our humanity from our praise and thanks, to our demands and laments are fully known and comprehended by God.

To grasp the difference between prayer as something answered and prayer as something understood, it is helpful to think of an analogy from human relationships. Imagine an occasion when you are going through a very difficult time, a tangled situation for which there is no solution. You pour out your heart to a friend who, with the best of intentions, tries to solve the unsolvable for you. Before your friend gets very far you interrupt to say, "I'm not looking for answers. I just want you to know what I'm going through. I just want to be understood."

If prayer is "something understood" and "Praying's the end of preaching," then the purpose of preaching is to give a sense of God's understanding presence in every circumstance of our lives. The purpose of preaching is to reassure us that we are understood by One "to whom all hearts are open, all desires known, and from whom no secrets are hid."

All of Us for All of God

Being understood takes many different forms. Think of the friend who laughs with you, shares your tears in sorrow, or gives just the look of assurance you need as you announce a major life decision. Because understanding takes a multitude of forms, it follows that preaching, if it is to nurture prayer as "something understood," needs to employ a wide repertoire of ways of knowing and communicating. "All of us for all of God" is the way James Ashbrook, a professor of pastoral theology and a colleague early in my career, used to put the matter. "All of us for all of God" is a principle manifest in the first and greatest commandment:

> "Hear, O Israel: the Lord our God, the Lord is one; you shall love the Lord your God with all your heart, and with all your soul, and with all your mind, and with all your strength." The second is this, "You shall love your neighbor as yourself." There is no other commandment greater than these. (Mark 12:29-31)

Since loving anyone includes the many ways we know and communicate with one another, filling the first commandment includes all the different ways we know and communicate with God, all the different ways we pray to God.

Preaching whose end is prayer aims at filling the first and greatest commandment, not just as individuals but also as a community. The commandment is addressed to the community of faith. It opens, "Hear, O Israel." Hear, O community of faith. We are to bring our whole selves to the act of corporate, public prayer. For the first commandment charges us to dedicate every faculty of our being to the love of God. Or as Henry Ward Beecher put the matter in his third series of lectures: "It is a love that is to be made up of all that there is in man."[1] All that there is in a woman. Such love does not favor heart over mind, or soul over strength. The commandment does not say, "Love me with all your heart and 50 percent of your mind or with all your soul and 50 percent of your strength."

Open to the Continuing Work of the Spirit

In the same spirit as the biblical commandment, Beecher, in his lecture of February 7, 1872, affirms the homiletical need to engage human beings in their entirety: "Preaching should be directed to every element of human nature that God has implanted in us,—to the imaginative, to the highly spiritual, to the moral, to that phase of the intellectual that works up and toward the invisible, and to the intellectual that works down to the material and tangible."[2] For Beecher, this means that preachers are not only to engage all the different cognitive capacities of the human mind but also to embrace all domains of knowledge, making sure not to limit themselves to the Bible alone. As profoundly as Beecher draws upon the Bible and affirms his faith in Christ, he wisely realizes that the Scriptures do not exhaust the wonder and glory of God, and that living faithfully requires us to stay open to the continuing work of the Holy Spirit: "I do not

1. Henry Ward Beecher, *Yale Lectures on Preaching*, three volumes in one (New York: Fords, Howard, & Hulbert, 1892), vol. III, 61.
2. Beecher, *Yale Lectures on Preaching*, vol. I, 60.

believe that the Bible contains all that it is necessary for a man to know of God. It was not designed that it should. Do you suppose that the Bible was meant to be a substitute for the revelation of the Holy Ghost?...The unfolding ages continually add to our knowledge of things."[3]

Beecher appeals to the Bible to affirm the necessity for openness to knowledge that extends beyond the limits of the Bible:

> It is a perversion to say that men are to preach nothing but the literal, textual Christ, or the literal, textual four Gospels, or the literal, textual Epistles; for all of life is open to you. You have a right to preach from everything, from the stars in the zenith to the lowest form of creation upon earth. All things belong to you, for you are Christ's. The earth is the Lord's and the fullness of it. The Lord is our Father, and therefore we are heirs.[4]

I find Beecher's words to be salutary for our own time and place in history, and especially for what it means to make praying the end of preaching in a society whose warring factions insist on reducing reality to their dominant ways of processing and understanding the world. The gracious character that is manifest through a life of prayer that embodies the greatest commandment is an antidote to the habits of thought fostered by ideology, scientism, and the idolizing of technology. These patterns of perception, cognition, and expression constrict human consciousness by asserting the supremacy of reason and defining the real as what is quantifiable. They do not require of us all our heart, all our soul, all our mind, all our strength, but only a truncated version of what God has created us to be. I now give three revealing examples of the distortions that arise from this diminishment of our humanity.

3. Beecher, *Yale Lectures on Preaching*, vol. III, 45–46.
4. Beecher, *Yale Lectures on Preaching*, vol. I, 80.

In a news article entitled "A Christian Apologist and an Atheist Thrive in an Improbable Bond," postdoctoral fellow at the medical school of the University of Pennsylvania Patrick Arsenault "attributed his ardor for his wife to 'neuronal change induced by mutual oxytocin release.'"[5] I do not question the science of the statement, and I appreciate having a more precise understanding of the biological and chemical basis of physical attraction. The statement, however, is an inadequate account of what it is in fact like to feel ardor for my wife. Even though I know and appreciate the science, I find the words "Darling, I love you" a much more complete way of expressing to my wife the affection and desire of my whole being than telling her that I am sensing "'neuronal change induced by mutual oxytocin release.'" Romance, passion, intermingling of bodies and souls are part of the joy of being a creature of God, and one of the functions of preaching is to celebrate these gifts by nurturing in us prayers of adoration and thanksgiving to the One who draws forth these gifts of the Spirit through the romantic imagination as well as through "'neuronal change induced by mutual oxytocin release.'"

Preaching whose end is praying helps us resist the diminishment of our humanity that is fostered not only by scientific reductionism but also by privileging a rationalist, data-driven view of reality above all other perspectives. In a review of *Dark Net*, a television series about unsettling digital phenomenon, the critic Neil Genzlinger recounts the story of a man who is obsessed with acquiring every kind of app. The man says on the show: "For me relationships are difficult. I see people as just a pile of information." Genzlinger goes on to observe that the man "compares data to heroin: Having it only makes you want more."[6]

5. *The New York Times* (October 4, 2014): A14.

6. Neil Genzlinger, "Exploring the Digital Age's Toll on Us," *New York Times* (January 21, 2016): C6.

Once people are reduced to being "just a pile of information," they can be commodified. Their identities become the commercially exploitable pattern of their internet searches. Preaching whose end is prayer can be a potent antidote to the data-driven diminishment of our humanity, especially when the end of preaching is to pray with all our heart, all our soul, all our mind, all our strength. By engaging the fullness of our humanity with the source and core of being that can never be digitized or quantified, prayer reveals that people are far more than "just a pile of information."

The Dangers of a Distorted Rationalism

Both of these examples—limiting the understanding of love to biochemical release and reducing our humanity to a pile of information—reflect a larger distorting rationalism that carries devastating results, especially for the poor and the marginalized.

Take, for example, a report about

the notorious skirmish between Lawrence H. Summers and José Lutzenberger, which happened on the sidelines of the Earth Summit in Rio de Janeiro in 1992....Mr. Summers, then chief economist of the World Bank, had lent his signature to a leaked memo making the case that poor countries would make an efficient dump for the trash of the rich. "The economic logic behind dumping a load of toxic waste in the lowest wage country is impeccable and we should face up to that," the memo argued. Mr. Lutzenberger...responded that Mr. Summers's reasoning "is perfectly logical but totally insane."[7]

---

7. Eduardo Porter, "In Latin America, Growth Trumps Climate," *New York Times* (December 10, 2014): B1.

"Perfectly logical but totally insane"—that is what happens when all the mind is used in isolation from all the heart, all the soul, and all the strength, and when all of them are not given to the One who is the source of justice and compassion. Preaching whose end is prayer leads to confession and repentance, as we acknowledge that our isolated rationality can too easily become "perfectly logical but totally insane."

If preachers are going to awaken such confession, they are going to have to understand the deeper roots of the diminishment of our God-given humanity. I find the work of Marcelo Gleiser—a professor of natural philosophy, physics, and astronomy at Dartmouth—very helpful in this homiletical task. In his book *The Island of Knowledge: The Limits of Science and the Search for Meaning*, Gleiser observes how science itself runs up against limits of what he terms "our information bubble."[8] These limits derive in part from the impact we have upon the phenomena we observe and the imperfection of our tools of measurement. In summary of his work, Gleiser cites Werner Heisenberg: "What we observe is not Nature itself but Nature exposed to our method of questioning."[9] No single scientific method nor the sum total of all our methods is sufficient for interpreting the wholeness of what we perceive and experience. We need some other way of imagining the deeper, higher, broader dimensions of the human situation in all its wonder and beauty, in all its brokenness and terror, in all its discontent and dreaming. To acknowledge this need for imagining the human situation in some frame more expansive than science alone is *not* to reject science nor to devalue its accomplishments. It is rather to celebrate those ineffable dimensions of human consciousness and feeling that make life profoundly satisfying.

8. Marcelo Gleiser, *The Island of Knowledge: The Limits of Science and the Search for Meaning* (New York: Basic Books, 2014), 94.

9. Gleiser, *The Island of Knowledge*, xiii.

Gleiser expresses both the limits of science and the riches of conscious existence in an extended meditation on the joy of human relationships. He begins by observing: "While the physical and social sciences surely can illuminate many aspects of knowledge, they shouldn't carry the burden of having all the answers. How small a view of the human spirit to cloister all that we can achieve in one corner of knowledge!"[10] I relish Gleiser's use of the word *cloister* here. It suggests that there can be a confining religious dogmatism to any form of human thought, including that of science. When "Praying's the end of preaching" and that praying embodies all our heart, all our soul, all our mind, and all our strength, then the human spirit is sprung lose from whatever solitary corner it is cloistered in.

Avoiding Cognitive Imperialism

Gleiser himself offers an alternative to cloistered thought through his observation: "We are multidimensional creatures and search for answers in many, complementary ways. Each serves a purpose, and we need them all." To recognize that we are "multidimensional creatures" and that we have many "complementary ways" of human knowing is to avoid what I term *cognitive imperialism*. Cognitive imperialism claims one form of human knowing to be the highest and most authoritative way of gaining knowledge, and it considers other forms of knowledge to be inferior at best and illusory at worst.

Although Gleiser himself does not use the term cognitive imperialism, he illustrates its meaning with a delightful analysis of a common human action:

10. This and the next two quotations are from Gleiser, *The Island of Knowledge*, 280–81.

Sharing a glass of wine with a loved one is more than just the chemistry of its molecular composition, the physics of its liquid consistency and the light reflections on its surface, or the biology of its fermentation and our sensorial response to it.

To all that we must add the experience of its ruby color and of its taste, the pleasure of the company, the twinkle in the eyes across the table, the quickening of the heart, the emotion of sharing the moment. Even if many of these reactions have a cognitive and neuronal basis, it would be a mistake to reduce them all to a measurable data set. It all sums up; it all becomes part of what it means to be alive, to search for answers, for companionship, for understanding, for love.

Although there are passages in Gleiser where he eschews any interest in theology, I find this passage implicitly theological in the way it moves from the purely physiological (the color of the wine, the processes of fermentation) to the realms of meaning, fellowship, and love—all of them central concerns of the gospel. In a manner Gleiser never intended, his description resonates with the sacrament of communion in which the church shares wine with its beloved Lord.

Science as a Source of Renewed Wonder and Doxology

Whatever Gleiser might think of my theological gloss on his scientific and philosophical ruminations, I believe he is addressing a hunger for a more holistic understanding of life. It is the very hunger that has drawn me to explore and expand upon George Herbert's assertion "Praying's the end of preaching." For I am convinced preaching can meet our hunger for a more integrated existence by nurturing a life of prayer that embodies the holistic spirit of the first and greatest commandment, and in doing so, reassures us that we are "understood." Such prayer mends the fragmentation of ourselves and our communities by personally relating the wholeness of who we are—heart and mind, soul and strength—to the deep, dear core of things, to the source of every good and perfect gift, to the one who created us, to the truth whose amplitude and complexity elude our most precise formulations and our profoundest art. But this mending and reclaiming of our full humanity cannot be achieved when we exclusively value one way of perceiving and processing reality above all others. The theologian and chemist Raimundo Panikkar writes: "The holistic attitude has been lost because the person has been reduced to reason, reason to intellect, and intellect to the ability to classify and to formulate laws about how things work."[11] When the full repertoire of prayer engages the full repertoire of our humanity—heart and mind and soul and strength—then we celebrate the gifts of science and reason while at the same time we are aware that no single mode of cognition is the only valid means of perceiving, processing, and responding to reality.

In his original lectures, Henry Ward Beecher expressed a sophisticated theological understanding of the importance and limitations of science and their significance for preaching: "Science is unpacking a particular part of the universe, and showing its infinite riches and variety and depth and complexity. All elements that go to make science so wonderful now are reacting in their turn, and are making that Divine Center who is the Father and Controller of these elements, still more wonderful."[12] Note the exactness of Beecher's observation. He does *not*

---

11. Raimundo Panikkar, *A Dwelling Place of Wisdom*, trans. Annemarie S. Kidder (Louisville: Westminster John Knox Press, 1993), 10, as quoted by Siroj Sorajjakool, *DO NOTHING: Inner Peace for Everyday Living: Reflections on Chuang Tzu's Philosophy* (West Conshohocken, PA: Templeton Foundation Press, 2009), 25.

12. Beecher, *Yale Lectures on Preaching*, vol. III, 119.

say: "Science is unpacking everything." He says: "Science is unpacking a *particular part* of the universe." Science has limits, but within those limits, Beecher considers it to be "wonderful." From his perspective, no preacher can afford to ignore science.

Beecher's interest in science grew not only out of his conviction about its theological significance but also out of a personal pastoral concern. Near the end of his third series of lectures he explains:

> I have a congregation which is filled with young scientists. I know their doubts. I am acquainted with their difficulties. I have for years been seeking to find out the way of presenting to them the truth as it is in Christs. . . . I have studied to impress men with the feeling that religion means that final form of development which consists in the perfect harmonization and strengthening of their powers around about a common center of the soul, under the Divine inspiration. . . . It has been my endeavor thus to gain the ear of men who were likely to be alienated from mere sectarian views which embrace philosophical formulas that are antiquated or run out.[13]

It is revealing to compare this quotation from Beecher's lecture, delivered March 18, 1874, with *The Christian Century* magazine issue of August 5, 2015. The magazine cover features a schematic picture of an atom and across the nucleus in capital letters is written the theme: SCIENCE IN THE CONGREGATION. In an article entitled "Scientists Welcome: A Challenge for Congregations," David J. Wood writes words to which Beecher would offer a hearty *Amen*: "To ignore the power of science to interpret the world is to impoverish theological reflection and leave unaddressed the lived experience of congregants."[14]

---

13. Beecher, *Yale Lectures on Preaching*, vol. III, 284–85.
14. David J. Wood, "Scientists Welcome: A Challenge for Congregations," *The Christian Century* (August 5, 2015): 23.

In an article that immediately follows Wood's, a number of pastors give testimony to their experience of cultivating conversation with scientists in their congregations. Wes Avram draws the following lessons from his experience:

> We need a new sense of wonder. Though I've experienced the church as a place where the most interesting questions are asked, scientists tell a different story. They speak of how their pull toward a career in science was like a calling, but their curiosity was silenced in church, as if it were a threat to their faith. We should have enough confidence in a creating and creative God to embrace a curiosity about how creation works.[15]

Science and reason have the capacity to awaken the sense of wonder for which Avram calls. It is a wonder that in turn feeds faith and prayer. David Wood gives a moving example of this:

> Xavier Le Pichon, a geophysicist who was instrumental in establishing the field of plate tectonics...talked about his experience descending to the floor of the Pacific Ocean in the early 1980s. At the time, it was the deepest depth attempted by a human being.
>
> He described the experience of descending to where the earth's crust is being constantly renewed as akin to being present at the moment of creation. The creatures that came into view, never before observed by a human being, exemplified their evolutionary character. Because of the intense darkness, there was no need for them to hide from predators: their colors were brilliant.
>
> Their bizarre shapes were adapted to the unique environment.
>
> For Le Pichon, the encounter was evocative: "I felt like Adam. For me, all I could do was pray and give thanks."

David Wood then reflects,

15. Wes Avram, "Congregational Conversations," *The Christian Century* (July 24, 2015): 27.

What gave his testimony such power was that it was a story of faith inextricably bound up with the passion of a scientist. His account had none of the triumphalist tone of efforts to show how science proves the existence of God. Rather, it was the testimony of a scientist experiencing God in the course of his discovery of nature. *And it was unequivocal doxology.*[16]

"Praying's the end of preaching" means, in a scientific age, that the task of preaching is in part to give witness to how science can awaken "unequivocal doxology." Such doxology is a way of loving God with all our heart, all our soul, all our mind, all our strength. When Le Pichon says, "I felt like Adam. For me, all I could do was pray and give thanks," he is not giving up his science or his reason but is allowing the totality of his humanity to be engaged by the phenomena that his science and reason have drawn him to observe. "Praying's the end of preaching" means in this day and age that the purpose of preaching is to engage the totality of our humanity with the same spirit that is manifest in the experience of Le Pichon.

The Centrality of the Preacher's Moral and Cognitive Character

How do we do that? How can preaching lead people to practice the full repertoire of prayer with the full repertoire of their humanity: with all their heart, all their soul, all their mind, all their strength? Homiletics is never able to avoid the "*how to* questions." Questions of method are inevitable to the discipline. But they bring with them a real danger— namely, that homiletics will be reduced to issues of language, organization, rhetoric, and the use of one's voice and body. The history of the

---

16. Wood, "Scientists Welcome: A Challenge for Congregations," 23 and 25, emphasis added.

Beecher lectures places these matters in a perspective that suggests if praying is to be the end of preaching then it will take something much more profound than rhetorical and vocal mastery.

Although many Beecher lecturers acknowledge and often give practical advice on the use of language and voice, they stress much more the development of the person of the preacher. When Batsell Barrett Baxter published his summary work on the Beecher lectures in 1947, he observed:

> There was no subject mentioned more often in the Lyman Beecher Lectures than that of the preacher's character. Twenty-nine [out of sixty-six][17] different lecturers mentioned its importance, thus giving it a place of primacy in the list of qualifications for effective preaching. Both by specific statement and by continuous repetition, the preacher's character was made the foundation upon which all else rises or falls.[18]

Here is a representative affirmation of the importance of character from the Beecher lecturer of 1909–1910, Charles E. Jefferson:

> In preaching it is the character of the preacher which is the preacher's power. Preaching is not a trick which can be mastered some bright morning, or a secret which can be transmitted from one man to another for a consideration.... All these things—voice, gesture, rhetoric, illustrations, quotations, ideas, learning—have a certain value, but they are at best superficialities, and all of them unless backed up by something better, soon grow thin and tame....Goodness never grows stale. Love never becomes monotonous.[19]

---

17. I derived the number of sixty-six from the following statement in Baxter's preface: "Begun in 1871, the lectures have been delivered each year through the seventy-seven-year period until the present date [1946], with the exception of four widely separated years. On several other occasions the lectures were delivered but never published. There are in existence at the present time sixty-six volumes of the famous series" (Batsell Barrett Baxter, *The Heart of the Yale Lectures* [New York: The Macmillan Company, 1947], vii–viii).

18. Baxter, *The Heart of the Yale Lectures*, 30–31.

19. Baxter, *The Heart of the Yale Lectures*, 35; originally appeared in Charles E. Jefferson, *The Building of the Church* (New York: The Macmillan Company, 1911), 282–86.

Certain traits of character have staying power in every time and place: goodness, integrity, compassion, fairness. The ancient rhetoricians, whose writings later influenced the development of Christian homiletics, taught that character was the first prerequisite for being an effective public speaker. Although the spin doctors of our social media age may make that ancient wisdom appear dated, I believe character is still essential to any ministry of preaching that will transform a community's corporate life over time.

When we speak about the character of a preacher, it is essential to understand that character includes more than the virtues of goodness, integrity, compassion, and fairness.

The *Oxford English Dictionary* defines *character* as "the sum of the moral and mental qualities which distinguish an individual or a people, viewed as a homogeneous whole; a person's or group's individuality deriving from environment, culture, experience, etc.; mental or moral constitution, personality."[20] Character concerns, then, not only our ethics but also our "mental qualities," our ways of knowing and communicating, our modes of cognition by which we perceive, process, and respond to the world.

Preaching that helps people to practice the full repertoire of prayer with all their heart, all their soul, all their mind, all their strength is preaching that shapes their mental qualities. It moves them beyond the reductionist thought impressed upon them by the distortions of ideology, scientism, and the obsessions of quantification and digitalization.

Therefore, preaching whose end is prayer is preaching that shapes character, not only the ethical content of character but also its habits of thought. In saying this, I do not mean to draw a rigid line between ethical content and habits of thought because, in fact, they are mutually

---

20. *Oxford English Dictionary*, "character": http://www.oed.com/view/Entry/30639?rskey=g2vyuo&result=1#eid.

interactive. Consider the story I related earlier about Lawrence Summers advocating that toxic waste be dumped upon marginalized peoples,
a proposal that José Lutzenberger described as "perfectly logical but totally insane." In this case the mental quality of isolated logic produced
egregious immorality. So when I say, "Preaching whose end is prayer is
preaching that shapes character," I mean the sum total of the interactive
dynamic between ethics and mental qualities.

That interactive dynamic is manifest in Christ's statement of the
two greatest commandments. It is significant that the scribe to whom
Christ is responding asks for only one commandment: "Which commandment is the first of all?" Christ gives him not one, but two, as if the
second spontaneously flowed from the first. The mental quality of loving
God with all our heart, all our soul, all our mind, all our strength gath-
ers momentum that moves inexorably to an ethic of compassion: "Love
your neighbor as yourself."

The interrelationship of the two commandments is especially clear in
Matthew's version because he connects them with the Greek word *homoia*,
whose first meaning in my Greek lexicon is "of the same nature."[21] Love of
neighbor is "of the same nature" as loving God with all our heart, all our
soul, all our mind, all our strength. Therefore, "Praying's the end of preaching" means that loving our neighbor as ourselves is the end of preaching.

"Praying's the end of preaching" turns out indeed to be a deceptively simple statement. The more we explore the principle the more
we realize that prayer is a comprehensive, multidimensional phenomenon that engages a wide repertoire of different modes of perceiving,
processing, and responding to the world. I believe this comprehensive

21. Walter Bauer, *A Greek-English Lexicon of the New Testament and Other Early Christian
Literature,* trans. William F. Arndt and F. Wilbur Gingrich (Chicago: The University of Chicago Press, 1957), 569.

understanding of prayer is close in spirit to what Paul the apostle has in mind when he writes to the Thessalonians and urges them to "pray without ceasing" (1 Thessalonians 5:17). Paul puts this command in the context of a number of instructions about the Thessalonians' common life, none of which they would have time to carry out if the words "pray without ceasing" bore the narrow, literal meaning "spend every minute in offering prayers to God." But if prayer has the broader, comprehensive meaning of living the fullest possible relationship to God and neighbor, then "pray without ceasing" includes living the life of mutual respect, love, patience, and goodness to which Paul exhorts the Thessalonians.

The full repertoire of public prayer in worship is a way of learning to incarnate the ceaseless prayer of living a life of justice and love in the world. Such holistic praying can only become the end of preaching when preachers nurture in themselves the gifts of character that flow from a vital relationship to God. Henry Ward Beecher in his first series of lectures identified this as an essential prerequisite for any ministry that would endure and be effective: "My impression is, that the fountain of strength in every Christian ministry is the power of the minister himself to realize God present, and to present him to the people. No ministry can be long, various, rich, and fruitful, I think, except from that root.... The preacher, then, must have the greatness of the God-power in his soul."[22]

Acknowledging and Correcting the Distortions of Religious Faith

Although I am convinced that "the God-power in [the] soul" is as essential to preaching as it ever was, I am also aware of how frightening

22. Beecher, *Yale Lectures on Preaching*, vol. I, 110–11.

this concept would sound to many people in the face of the violence and hatred perpetuated by religious believers who are convinced they have the absolute truth about God. For these good reasons many might well argue against "the God-power in [the] soul" and forcefully reject the idea of all of us for all of God, pointing to century after century of persecution, torture, and warfare carried out in the name of divinity. Even though I have deep faith in God, I believe the church must take seriously and appreciatively why many people are hostile to religion and fearful of any talk of God. My response to such people is that violence and hatred in the name of God are the result of our failure to live up to the first and greatest commandments. Instead of loving God with all our heart, all our soul, all our mind, all our strength, we engage only a portion of what we are created to be and thus distort our humanity and our understanding of God. We lose the mutually correcting and counterbalancing effect of engaging our full selves with the deep, dear core of things whose possibilities always exceed our calculations, and who thereby nurtures the openness to others that precludes raining violence upon them under the pretense of carrying out the divine will. "Praying's the end of preaching" includes, then, acknowledging religion's violent history and cultivating communities of faith who demonstrate through their common life that giving all of us to all of God brings mending and peace.

To give all aspects of our humanity to the One who created us and whom we recognize as the source of truth is to energize the whole repertoire of prayer with the whole repertoire of our humanity. Some critics may object that when "Praying's the end of preaching," the church will replace reliance upon the Bible with the instabilities and foibles of human subjectivity. People will mistake the voice of their own ego for the voice of the Spirit. Yes, that is always a danger, but it is equally a danger when exposition of the Bible is the purpose of preaching, for the process of interpretation is as liable to the distortions of human subjectivity as prayer. Beecher is helpful here. He likens biblical interpretation to the physical labor of mining and forging:

> We never find, in the natural world, knives and lancets to our hands; but we find there the ore out of which steel is made for their manufacture. In the natural world we find the raw material for the supply of our physical wants; and it is our business to take this raw material and work it up.... The Bible is a great book stored with much that is beautiful and valuable, and which men can gain by digging and working it, as ore from a mine, but in no other way.[23]

Sometimes, however, people mine and forge the wrong things from the Bible. Think of all the times people have mined the Scriptures to find justification for slavery, for blocking science, for the subjugation of women, for racism, for the condemnation of homosexuality.

And even when people are mining from the Bible what is "beautiful and valuable," there is always the possibility that the Word will come out diminished and distorted. John Collins offers a helpful analysis of why this happens: "The Bible has contributed to violence in the world precisely because it has been taken to confer a degree of certitude that transcends human discussion and argumentation. Perhaps the most constructive thing a biblical critic can do toward lessening the contribution of the Bible to violence in the world is to show that such certitude is an illusion."[24] As profoundly as I appreciate the contribution of biblical

---

23. Beecher, *Yale Lectures on Preaching*, vol. III, 15.
24. John J. Collins, *Does the Bible Justify Violence?* (Minneapolis: Fortress Press, 2004), 32–33.

critics to preaching, I believe that it will require not only scholarship but also the practice of prayer that I have traced in this book to lessen the destructive certitude that has flowed from misusing the Bible. Prayer keeps us in relationship with the One to whom the Bible gives witness and who is even greater than the Bible itself. When we bring all of us to all of God in prayer, one of the first things we realize is how finite we are and how limited our knowledge is. We become aware that we understand far less than we are understood—an awareness that nurtures a posture of soul, an inclination of the mind, an openness in the heart that is far less prone to the certitude on which violence feeds.

There is no foolproof way to avoid the misuse of the Bible. Nevertheless, when we earthen creatures risk such an audacious act as preaching in the name of God, we lessen the chances of theological distortion if we practice a broad repertoire of prayer in a community of faith that employs the full repertoire of our humanity, a community that embodies loving God with all our heart, all our soul, all our mind, all our strength, and our neighbors as ourselves. As Herbert instructed us in "The Church-Porch":

Though private prayer be a brave design,

Yet public hath more promises, more love:

And love's a weight to hearts, to eyes a sign.

We all are but cold suitors; let us move

> *Where it is warmest. Leave thy six and seven;*

> *Pray with the most: for where most pray, is heaven.*[25]

25. George Herbert, *The Complete English Poems*, ed. John Tobin (London: Penguin Books, 1991), 19, stanza 67.

Chapter Three

If the end of preaching is prayer, then how will we arrive at that end? The only way to arrive there is to begin there. The end of preaching is prayer, and the beginning of preaching is prayer.

So let us pray in word and song.

> *Source of all wonder,*
>
> *wellspring of living waters,*
>
> *womb of being,*
>
> *Mother/Father, creator of all,*
>
> *our beginning and our end,*
>
> *we pray*
>
> *that you will continually renew our relationship to you,*
>
> *through heart and soul and mind and strength*
>
> *so that we your preachers*
>
> *may manifest in our sermons*
>
> *and in our very being and acting*
>
> *the abundance of life that people can enjoy,*
>
> *the new creation they can become*
>
> *and the restored world they can fashion*
>
> *through the empowerment of*
>
> *the Spirit and the risen Christ. AMEN.*

Lord, Keep Us Modest When We Claim

Lord, keep us modest when we claim
to know your heart's desires
lest we invoke you to inflame
belief's destructive fires.
Let it suffice that we should find
the star-stitched quilt of night
a marvel that provokes our mind
to seek yet deeper light.

From wonder let more wonder flow
at how the atom spins,
how cells are formed, evolve and grow,
how life itself begins,
how mass and energy give rise
to yearnings in our hearts
that reach beyond the farthest skies
for where existence starts.

Then let our yearning hearts become
an open door to prayer,
a way to hear your Spirit hum
through words and acts of care,
a way to stretch our self-concern
beyond our routine course,
a way to live that helps us learn
you are life's end and source.

And let these simple, prayerful ways
dispel the violence bred
when faith is turned from thanks and praise
to hatred, fear and dread.
Yet even more may prayer make clear
faith's universal claim:
you hold the whole creation dear,
and love is your true name.[26]

---

26. Thomas H. Troeger, unpublished, copyright 2015, Oxford University Press.

www.ingramcontent.com/pod-product-compliance
Lightning Source LLC
Chambersburg PA
CBHW010857090426
42737CB00020B/3411